I0463358

Catch Your
Plot Bunnies

A journal to capture your next great
book idea before it hops away.

A great book would be ...

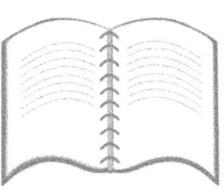

_____

_____

_____

_____

_____

_____

_____

_____

_____

_____

_____

Priority ☆☆☆

A great book would be ...

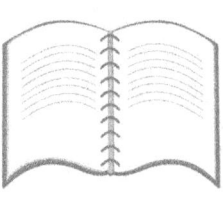

_____
_____
_____
_____
_____
_____
_____
_____
_____
_____
_____

Priority ☆☆☆

A great book would be ...

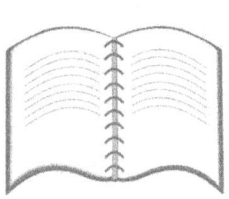

_____

_____

_____

_____

_____

_____

_____

_____

_____

_____

Priority

A great book would be ...

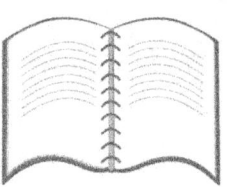

_____

_____

_____

_____

_____

_____

_____

_____

_____

_____

Priority ☆☆☆

A great book would be ...

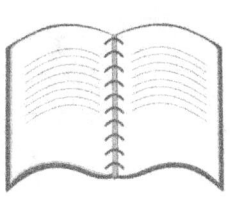

_____

_____

_____

_____

_____

_____

_____

_____

_____

Priority ☆☆☆

A great book
would be ...

_____

_____

_____

_____

_____

_____

_____

_____

_____

_____

Priority ☆☆☆

A great book would be ...

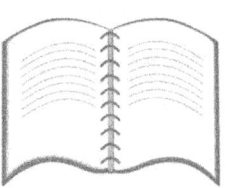

_____

_____

_____

_____

_____

_____

_____

_____

_____

_____

_____

Priority ☆☆☆

A great book would be ...

Priority ☆☆☆

A great book would be …

Priority ☆☆☆

A great book would be ...

_____

_____

_____

_____

_____

_____

_____

_____

_____

_____

Priority ☆☆☆

A great book would be ...

_____

_____

_____

_____

_____

_____

_____

_____

_____

_____

_____

Priority ☆☆☆

A great book would be ...

_____

_____

_____

_____

_____

_____

_____

_____

_____

_____

Priority ☆☆☆

A great book would be ...

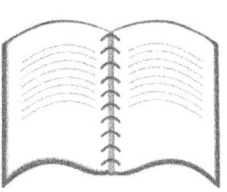

_____

_____

_____

_____

_____

_____

_____

_____

_____

_____

_____

Priority ☆☆☆

A great book would be ...

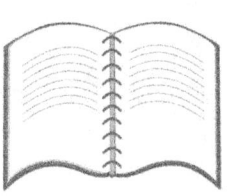

Priority ☆☆☆

A great book would be ...

_____

_____

_____

_____

_____

_____

_____

_____

_____

_____

_____

Priority ☆☆☆

A great book would be ...

_____

_____

_____

_____

_____

_____

_____

_____

_____

_____

_____

Priority ☆☆☆

A great book would be ...

Priority ☆☆☆

A great book would be ...

Priority ☆☆☆

A great book

would be ...

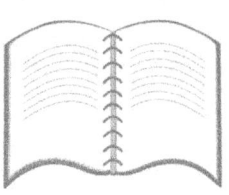

Priority ☆☆☆

A great book would be ...

_____

_____

_____

_____

_____

_____

_____

_____

_____

_____

Priority ☆☆☆

A great book would be ...

_____

_____

_____

_____

_____

_____

_____

_____

_____

_____

Priority ☆☆☆

A great book would be ...

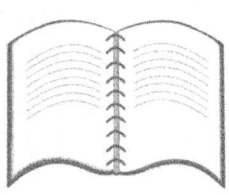

_____

_____

_____

_____

_____

_____

_____

_____

_____

_____

_____

Priority ☆☆☆

A great book would be ...

_____

_____

_____

_____

_____

_____

_____

_____

_____

_____

Priority ☆☆☆

A great book would be ...

_____

_____

_____

_____

_____

_____

_____

_____

_____

_____

Priority ☆☆☆

A great book would be ...

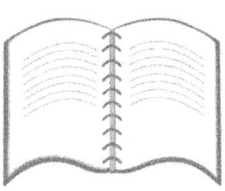

_____

_____

_____

_____

_____

_____

_____

_____

_____

_____

Priority ☆☆☆

A great book would be ...

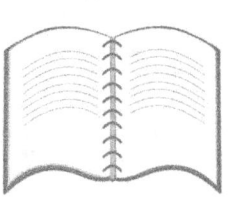

Priority ☆☆☆

A great book
would be ...

_____

_____

_____

_____

_____

_____

_____

_____

_____

Priority ☆☆☆

A great book would be ...

_____

_____

_____

_____

_____

_____

_____

_____

_____

_____

_____

_____

Priority ☆☆☆

A great book would be ...

Priority ☆☆☆

A great book would be ...

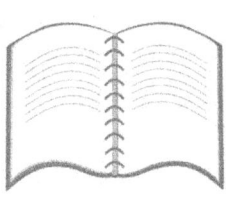

_____

_____

_____

_____

_____

_____

_____

_____

_____

_____

Priority ☆☆☆

A great book would be ...

_____

_____

_____

_____

_____

_____

_____

_____

_____

_____

_____

Priority ☆☆☆

A great book would be ...

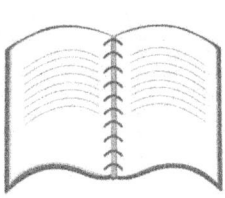

_____

_____

_____

_____

_____

_____

_____

_____

_____

_____

_____

Priority ☆☆☆

A great book would be ...

Priority ☆☆☆

A great book would be ...

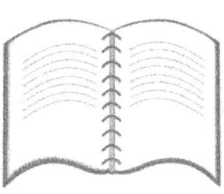

_____

_____

_____

_____

_____

_____

_____

_____

_____

_____

Priority ☆☆☆

A great book would be ...

_____

_____

_____

_____

_____

_____

_____

_____

_____

_____

Priority ☆☆☆

A great book would be ...

Priority ☆☆☆

A great book would be ...

Priority ⭐☆☆

A great book would be ...

Priority ☆☆☆

A great book would be ...

_____

_____

_____

_____

_____

_____

_____

_____

_____

_____

Priority

A great book would be ...

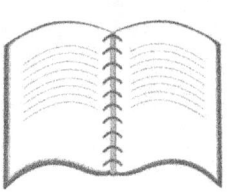

_____

_____

_____

_____

_____

_____

_____

_____

_____

_____

_____

Priority ☆☆☆

A great book would be ...

_____

_____

_____

_____

_____

_____

_____

_____

_____

_____

Priority ☆☆☆

A great book would be ...

_____

_____

_____

_____

_____

_____

_____

_____

_____

_____

_____

Priority ☆☆☆

A great book would be ...

_____

_____

_____

_____

_____

_____

_____

_____

_____

_____

_____

Priority ☆☆☆

A great book would be ...

Priority ☆☆☆

A great book
would be …

_____

_____

_____

_____

_____

_____

_____

_____

_____

_____

Priority ☆☆☆

A great book would be ...

_____

_____

_____

_____

_____

_____

_____

_____

_____

_____

Priority ☆☆☆

A great book would be ...

_____

_____

_____

_____

_____

_____

_____

_____

_____

_____

Priority ☆☆☆

A great book would be ...

_____

_____

_____

_____

_____

_____

_____

_____

_____

_____

Priority

A great book would be ...

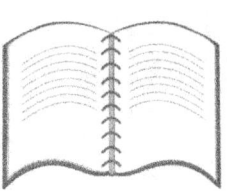

Priority ☆☆☆

A great book would be ...

_____

_____

_____

_____

_____

_____

_____

_____

_____

_____

Priority ☆☆☆

A great book would be ...

_____

_____

_____

_____

_____

_____

_____

_____

_____

_____

Priority ☆☆☆

A great book would be ...

Priority ☆☆☆

A great book would be ...

Priority ☆☆☆

A great book
would be ...

_____

_____

_____

_____

_____

_____

_____

_____

_____

Priority ☆☆☆

A great book would be ...

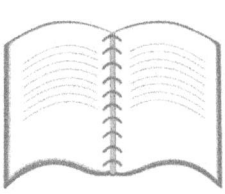

_____

_____

_____

_____

_____

_____

_____

_____

_____

_____

Priority ☆☆☆

A great book would be ...

Priority ☆☆☆

A great book would be ...

_____

_____

_____

_____

_____

_____

_____

_____

_____

_____

Priority

A great book would be ...

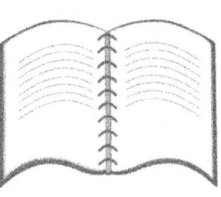

_____

_____

_____

_____

_____

_____

_____

_____

_____

_____

Priority ☆☆☆

A great book would be ...

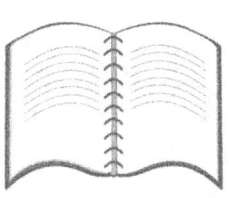

Priority ☆☆☆

A great book would be ...

_____

_____

_____

_____

_____

_____

_____

_____

_____

_____

Priority ☆☆☆

A great book would be ...

Priority ☆☆☆

A great book would be ...

Priority ☆☆☆

A great book

would be ...

_____

_____

_____

_____

_____

_____

_____

_____

_____

_____

Priority ☆☆☆

A great book would be ...

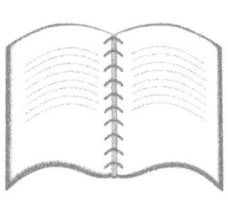

Priority ☆☆☆

A great book would be ...

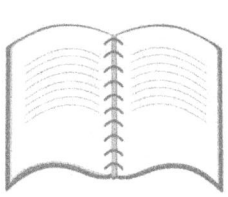

Priority ☆☆☆

A great book would be ...

_____

_____

_____

_____

_____

_____

_____

_____

_____

_____

Priority ☆☆☆

A great book would be ...

_____

_____

_____

_____

_____

_____

_____

_____

_____

_____

_____

Priority ☆☆☆

A great book would be ...

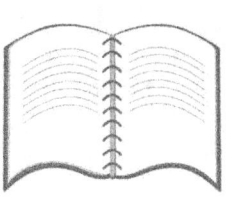

_____

_____

_____

_____

_____

_____

_____

_____

_____

_____

_____

Priority ☆☆☆

A great book
would be ...

Priority ☆☆☆

A great book
would be ...

_____
_____
_____
_____
_____
_____
_____
_____
_____
_____

Priority ☆☆☆

A great book would be ...

_____

_____

_____

_____

_____

_____

_____

_____

_____

_____

Priority ☆☆☆

A great book would be ...

Priority ☆☆☆

A great book would be ...

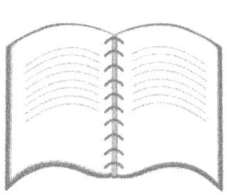

Priority ⭐⭐⭐

A great book would be ...

Priority ☆☆☆

A great book would be ...

Priority ☆☆☆

A great book would be ...

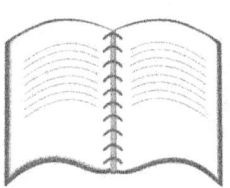

Priority ☆☆☆

A great book would be ...

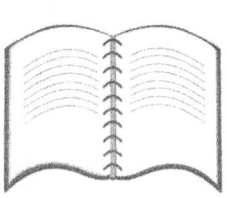

Priority ☆☆☆

A great book would be …

Priority ☆☆☆